we can see your privates

we can see your privates

Presented by The House of Haiku

MrJeffDess

grew bap books New York 2011

grew bap books
Brooklyn, New York

ISBN: 978-1-257-86711-0

Also by MrJeffDess
do not hold doors
haiku from the home of reverend mofo jones

MOFO JONES TELEGRAM GROUP

The filing time shown in the date line on telegrams and day letters is STANDARD TIME at point of origin.

BK NY June 17 422pm   from the house of haiku

You are receiving this telegram because it is officially time to investigate. The private life has infiltrated the public with more vigor and ferocity then has ever been experienced before. Exposure has the community inebriated. Thus, leaving the line between public and private a blurry and disorganized mess. Habitual line stepping across the world is at an all time high. The public opinion has been co-opted. Definitions of censorship and freedom of speech are now blown all over that brown Brougham.

The "public sphere" as coined by Jürgen Habermas is a funky space. It encourages excellent opportunities to exchange views and express opinions. Public thoughts shared open the door to some of the finest collaborative prospects in the land. The private is looking to take complete control.

Within us exists secret thoughts that are itching to get out. It is our responsibility not to scratch. There are certain hush – hush desires looking for that one shot to blurt out what's wrong in a world filled with a confusing amount of rights and lefts. These escape efforts must be thwarted.

-MrJeffDess

MOFO JONES TELEGRAM GROUP

The filing time shown in the date line on telegrams and day letters is STANDARD TIME at point of origin.

BK NY June 18 632pm   **from the house of haiku**

Today's major culprits include but are not limited to the following: Reality Television, Social Media, The current pulse of the music industry, Political Discourse and Treatment of personal relationships. Please be on the lookout.

If the community seeks to effectively discuss culture, lifestyle, politics and other societal entities, a clearer separation of the public and private is necessary. For the sake of critique it is necessary for certain aspects of the private sphere that should be brought to light. As a community we have gone too far. We are moonwalking very close to the edge. Trust and believe that the fall will be an ugly one.

Together we must retreat to the HOUSE OF HAIKU. The haiku found within THE HOUSE OF HAIKU will do the investigating. They will look deeply at language and life that define the public and private. If you are able to navigate your way through THE HOUSE OF HAIKU, you will be safe. If not, someone may very well show your privates to the public.

-MrJeffDess

MOFO JONES TELEGRAM GROUP

The filing time shown in the date line on telegrams and day letters is STANDARD TIME at point of origin.

BK NY June 22 517pm   from the house of haiku

Please be aware of the following individuals and/or groups. They have been overwhelmed by the current blurring of lines. They are amongst the many to be overtaken by the confusion.

Anthony Weiner
Kim Kardashian
Tracy Morgan
John Edwards
TMZ.com
Mel Gibson
The Cast of Basketball Wives
Chris Brown
Your future ex-girlfriend
The man picking his nose at the dinner table
The youth of today and tomorrow

Post Script: Telegrams were used because no other means of current communication are private.

-MrJeffDess

For Reference:

THE HOUSE OF HAIKU is an organ. THE HOUSE OF HAIKU is a platform. In a world filled with manipulation, THE HOUSE OF HAIKU is one of the few constant connectors to reality. THE HOUSE OF HAIKU is a tool of deconstruction. THE HOUSE OF HAIKU will challenge your mind and spirit. All visitors to THE HOUSE OF HAIKU must leave their cool at the door. It is recommended that you do not wipe your feet upon entry into THE HOUSE OF HAIKU.

THE HOUSE OF HAIKU never closes. NEVER.

The broad array of citizens' voices is channeled through a narrow runnel of market – driven mass – media outlets, grossly limiting the public presentation of popular sentiment

Cornel West
Democracy Matters

my vote is private

1
**Can't afford college.
Go to Afghanistan. No
more debt but I'm dead**

2
**The banks being bailed
out. Will somebody bail me
out from Sallie Mae?**

3
Fight for my country.
When I return home they are
not fighting for me.

4
Can you truly win
a war if your enemy
is not scared of death?

5
Fighting wars against
invisible enemies.
My vision is veiled.

6
So osama bin
laden is dead but I still
cannot find a job

7
I would like george bush
to produce his report cards
and college transcripts

8
Electing a black
president revealed a lot
of racist feelings

9
Economy has
been grounded and will not come
out to play with us

10
Capitalism
is a dangerous beast that
will eat anything

11
Privatized prisons
profit and pump pockets then
punish prisoners

12
Incarcerated
scarfaces are people too.
End all the abuse

13
I voted for you
to lead but you chose to show
her your dick instead

14
If your mayor did
a good job but cheated on
their spouse would you care?

15
Hugh Hefner can still
get married but gay people
still don't have the right

16
I asked. You told. Yet
you were still able to save
me from terrorists

17
The democrats and
republicans fight more than
the bloods and the crips

18
The democratic
party and democracy
are not the same thing

19
How did we as a
people let sarah palin
get to this level?

20
If elected don't
worry I won't keep any
of my promises

21
Voices arguing
Afghanistan. Unemployed.
Silent death marches

22
My president is
black and so was the water
found in the gulf coast

In the institution of art criticism, including literary, theater and music criticism, the lay judgment of a public that had come of age, or at least thought it had, became organized.

Jurgen Habermas
The Structural Transformation of the Public Sphere

it's a public society all we ask is trust

23
**Is knowing how to
roll an L more important
than the honor roll?**

24
**It's hard out there for
a pimp but even harder
for educators**

25
What the fuck do I
care about community?
I need that paper

26
The guy who picks up
my trash makes more than the guy
who runs my country

27
Sometimes I wish the
bodega sold books instead
of beer and bogeys

28
You want to know where
the wild things really are? Check
the housing projects

29
In the projects the
biggest terrorists are the
cops and crack dealers

30
Before there were new
kids on the block there were grown
ass men on the block

31
A black man has a
better chance of catching a
court case than a cab

32
When I entered the
elevator she grabbed her
purse out of pure fear

33
Losing internet
is not a tragedy it's
a first world problem

34
Teen violence and
Healthcare system. Poverty
and Education

35
Domestic Abuse
AIDS Capitalism war
Genocide Cancer

36
Homophobia
Racism Classism Crime
The Environment

37
America eats
its young then complains about
having weight problems

38
We've become vultures
happily eating dinner
with other vultures

39
This world would be a
better place if there were just
a few less assholes

40
Homo sapiens
who still say no homo need
to do their homework

41
Colossal oil spills.
Arnold Schwarzenegger's love
child. Which tale means more?

42
Trying to make some
bread while waiting on line for
some government cheese

43
Is it possible
to feed sharks when all they want
to do is eat you?

44
Sheep in sheep's clothing.
No knowledge of where to go
next. Just following

45
We don't pick cotton
anymore but instead we
pick on each other

46
Critique of the real
life issues. You say nothing
watching with mouths shut

Everybody wanna be a nigga; but nobody wanna be a nigga.

Paul Mooney

public school #92

47
Children are acting
like adults. Adults thinking
that they're still children

48
At what pace do you
expect me to grow up? What
an amazing race.

49
Grade 2 should be more
about hugs and homework than
about homicide

50
Are you willing to
sacrifice and risk for the
sake of the babies?

51
The goals of some cops
in my hood is to make sure
I don't see 18

52
Some boys from the hood
grow up to be gentleman
who help out the hood

53
If her sidekick is
a sidekick than she's likely
too young for you sir

54
Kids are having sex
at a younger age and we
share some of the blame

55
Mentality and
age limits are colliding
at a scary pace

56
Have you checked in on
your babies? They have grown up
and are checking out.

57
I do not listen
to my teacher because she
is afraid of me

58
Not ready for the
next level because teachers
didn't prepare me

59
Respect has vanished
let me do me and I shall
figure out the rest

60
Their faces scarred by
the reality that we
introduced to them

61
Do all those kids that
break dance on the train all day
ever go to school?

62
These young brothers need
a new hero that doesn't
rap or play some ball

63
Cats care more about
their philly blunts than learning
about their phonics

64
No white picket fence.
The grass was not greener. The
concrete jungle roared

65
Her american
dream contained nothing but big
old scary monsters

66
We riot because
you are refusing to hear
our tremendous voice

The capacity for fantasy becomes the crucial function in the ability to finally overthrow reality and the displeasures that accompany it, to unleash desire in truly non – repressive situations of gratification and joy

Paul Garon
Blues and the Poetic Spirit

private access television

67
Basketball wives. Mob
wives. Real Housewives where are all
the husbands and kids?

68
Fuck the real housewives
of Atlanta how bout the
real homeless of Queens

69
How can you keep up
with the kardashians but
not your cable bill?

70
The next season of
survivor should take place in
the marcy projects

71
The man who versus
food should start feeding the man
who versus hunger

72
The biggest loser
has been my community's
development. Hope.

73
The O.J. Simpson
murder case changed the way we
watched television

74
What was once a need
to know basis is now a
need to show basis

75
Now that oprah's gone
where is a brother to find
his true emotions?

76
Maybe one day I
too will find true love on a
reality show

77
The revolution
will be televised if you
buy 3D glasses

78
3D movies do
nothing but give me headaches
and eat my wallet

79
It's 10 o'clock. Do
you know where your children are?
Watching bad TV

80
After you finish
your homework. Maybe I will
let you watch TV

81
Educated and
18 would be better than
16 and pregnant

82
When Brenda had her
baby did MTV film
all the happenings?

83
Snooki and Toni
Morrison. What do these two
gals have in common?

84
America's best
dance crew meet america's
best educators

85
Creative image.
Tortured by the changing of
the many channels

86
Six million ways to
die yet eight million tv
shows to choose to watch

Everybody wanna go to heaven but nobody wants to die.

Andre 3000
Rollin

holding hands in public

87
As you walk away
I keep hoping that you'll turn
around one more time

88
she cheated on me.
Now I wonder if she should
get another shot

89
Sometimes people go
on great dates but have poor sex
It will be okay

90
Once you find yourself
in the friend zone chances of
getting out are slim

91
If you're the other
woman you may want to Re-
examine your role

92
At the end of the
day cheating on her was not
worth all the hassle

93
Public displays of
affection are fine. public
displays of sex. Not.

94
Courting a lady
should be eventful. not a
televised event

95
We used to call to
say I love you now we text
to say I like you

96
Do not prolong the
relationship that's a break
up in the making

97
I turned to hug you.
Skirt back on. hair wrapped with one
foot out of the door

98
There's a reason why
she is called wifey and you
are called the side chick

99
Fantasies of your
footsteps tap dancing on my
heart are still haunting

100
We're speaking the same
language but no one knows what's
really going on

101
Cuddle with my boo
in the winter. Roam free as
a bird in the spring

102
I don't know why I
took your number I have no
intentions to call

103
I masturbate on
a regular basis and
my girl doesn't know

104
You were the hottest
beauty until we had that
first conversation

105
Don't front as if you
care about me, we both know
this is just some sex

106
Did you have sex on
the first date without knowing
your partner's last name?

107
I took a risk and
dialed. Listened to your voice.
Went silent. Hung up.

108
Although you've left. The
scent of your spirit remains.
Holding me hostage.

109
Can I kiss you while
others are watching? Are we
wrong for doing this?

110
This relationship
will never happen because
you showed me too much

People like seeing their name in print, or hearing their name. It's music! It makes them feel important, and people like to feel important. That's the normal, natural way of humanity.

Ron Galella

privately celebrating

111
Celebrate the seen
and pay no attention to
those that need it most

112
True success will take
more than 15 minutes of
fame and exposure

113
**The talentless are
getting more praise than those with
great talent and skill**

114
**Who needs school when you
could have just made a freaky
sex tape to succeed?**

115
There is rehab for
drug and sex addicts but not
for stupidity

116
Face tattoos are a
recipe for disaster
and unemployment

117
I pledge allegiance
to your flash and the pictures
that you'll show to them

118
I am a private
person in a public light
searching for sunsets

119
If I look good what
does it matter if the whole
world sees my goodies?

120
Your average backup
quarterback doesn't grow up
to marry models

121
Do we anoint our
heroes to a level that
can never be reached?

122
At a point the state
of ohio will have to
get over lebron

123
Your swag is at a
million but your bank account
is twenty dollars

124
Everyone and their
mama want to start clothing
lines. Souls stay naked

125
It's really none of
my business who kanye west
has sex with or dates

126
Knowledge of chris brown's
birthday. No knowledge of when
martin was murdered.

127
The stars have aligned
and the paparazzi has
smothered the brightness

128
The hills are alive
with the sound of musical
death and destruction

129
Voices of teachers
should ring louder than any
lady gaga song

130
He's been taught how to
dougie but has he been taught
how to multiply?

131
Sometimes I think that
there is just one rapper too
many in this world.

132
On this day one can
become a musical star
without leaving home

133
Something I learned from
rap songs is that you can rhyme
nigga with nigga

134
Signed contracts and iced
out nooses with skinny jeans.
singin and dancin

135
The men who run rap
have no problem lynching rap.
They've done so before

136
There's no reason that
I know the ingredients
of crack. Thanks Rick Ross

137
Who needs song writing?
My goal is to lead a dance
dance revolution

138
I wanted to be
loved. Compromised my beliefs
nobody loves me

139
Who needs to have strong
vocals and soul when your ass
moves in such a way?

140
Crashing into my
mental. Dangerously changed
lanes with not a care.

141
My american
idol can't sing but wishes
to change the country

142
I have given you
too much of my attention.
you took advantage

Finally, each man, in giving himself to all, gives himself to nobody.

Jean-Jacques Rousseau
On the Social Contract

publicly minding my own business

143
Your most authentic
self will be revealed when no
one is noticing

144
I've fallen into
a dark unfamiliar place
I am truly scared

145
I'm not as smart as
you but I have a lot more
swagger than you do

146
If everyone is
cool and trendy then no one
is cool and trendy

147
At the end of the
day we all have a little
paul pfieffer in us

148
I remember the
days of stealing mad strings off
of people's jansports

149
I took steroids to
get hot girls and instead I
got diabetes

150
I watch all dat azz
videos on tuesday and
thursday afternoons

151
I can never find
a band aid that matches the
color of my skin

152
The itch followed by
blissful joy next to immense
pain. I need you now

153
Dear lord if I am
to survive this hangover
I won't drink again

154
Too many glasses
of henny can make a man
think he's cassius clay

155
My life is extra
crispy and original
recipe in one

156
If you take enough
pictures of me maybe you'll
see into my soul

157
I am who I am
the darkness has deep love for
the truth within me

158
I was scared of the
boogeyman until he had
fun in my nightmare

159
We illegally
Cracked open the fire hyrdrant
Shower me with gifts.

160
When duane reade and the
block are both closed where am I
to get my good drugs?

161
Between me and you
I like wearing underwear
with dickholes in em

162
At the end of the
day we're all weirdos in the
eyes of someone else

163
When we didn't have
heat we would open up the
oven door for warmth

164
We didn't have the
lawn or the water for a
legit slip and slide

165
We don't have the same
opinion. that doesn't mean
I'm hating on you

166
I knew some boys from
my hood who cried at the end
of boyz in the hood

Now when I came out I told you all it was just about Biggie then everybody had to open their mouth with a motherfucking opinion

Tupac Shakur
Hit em up

no more privacy settings

167
Privacy setting
on social media is
an oxymoron

168
Certain photographs
should never be posted up
on the internet

169
What will happen when
the smart phone becomes smarter
then the rest of us?

170
Wrist bone connected
to the cell phone. The cell phone
connects to your life

171
You look better in
your profile picture than you
do in your tagged ones

172
People are a lot
tougher from behind a lap-
top than in person

173
Big brother may not
be watching us but he has
checked in on Foursquare

174
The day my mother
joins facebook is the day I
will delete facebook

175
I've got an App for
angry birds now I need one
for my depression

176
My new Ipad will
cure my boredom but it will
not cure my cancer?

177
Too much coverage.
Too much information. I
surrender to you

178
My cell phone won't cause
cancer because it never
has any service

179
If you didn't read
about it first on twitter
it didn't happen

180
I am nobody.
my internet connections
make me somebody

181
**We have the right to
information but how much
info is too much?**

182
**Who needs mentors when
you have over a thousand
loyal facebook friends?**

183
I can blog with the
best of them. But I still need
to learn how to write

184
I have forgotten
how to speak but I can text
with the best of them

185
They won't speak to your
face but they will text about
you behind your back

186
Social media
Socially awkward. So shall
we text talk or tweet?

187
I followed you on
twitter and you led me to
my own destruction

188
Pictures of me drunk
found on the internet. I
did not get the job

189
Use your camera phone
to catch brutality not
just fun youtube clips

190
Skype. G Chat. Twitter.
Text message. Facebook. Face Time.
I don't need to call.

"Why do you laugh?" he said. *"Because at a price I now see that which I couldn't see."*

Excerpt from Ralph Ellison's Invisible Man

have you seen your privates?

191
What does a leader
look like? What sounds do they make?
Are you a leader?

192
How can I cross the
line when the line keeps changing
its identity?

193
Is anyone else
through seeing little girls pop
it like beyonce?

194
Are you a hater
but thinks it's all good because
it's done on the low?

195
How many of you
are watching porn and ashamed
to admit the truth?

196
How does one find an
answer if the multiple
choices are endless?

197
Feed me and fuck me
feel me and free me but do
you really love me?

198
What if teachers were
paid the same salary as
alex rodriguez?

199
If a tree falls and
there's no paparazzi to
catch it. Did it fall?

200
How can you be that
poor yet own so many shoes
What is the next step?

201
How many people
hate their day jobs but still need
to pay the damn bills?

202
You satisfy my
body but can you ever
satisfy my soul?

203
Do you remember
How scary getting lost was
before GPS?

204
Is it ever fine
for a grown straight man to whip
his hair back and forth?

205
You go hard in the
muthafuckin paint but have
you done your homework?

206
Can you name a few
basketball wives but not a
supreme court justice?

207
Did the new season
premiere get you more hyped than
dreams of the future?

208
Why would you ever
post that picture if you did
not want my comments?

209
Where in the world is
carmen sandiego and
has she seen my dad?

210
How many numbers
have you drunk texted over
the last month or so?

211
I can't afford gas.
I can't afford insurance
Why am I driving?

212
Should I be allowed
to send out explicit pics
without you knowing?

213
We laughed. We kissed. We
even had lobster but why
won't you call me back?

214
If she swallows will
you respect her or just tell
your boys the next day?

215
Am I allowed to
do what I want if you do
not know about it?

216
What are we watching?
When will we be able to
watch it together?

You are always welcome back to the House of Haiku.

MrJeffDess aka Jeffrey Dessources is a writer, emcee and professor of Haitian descent. He received his M.A. in English Literature from St. John's University and he is the author of the texts do not hold doors and Haiku from the Home of Reverend Mofo Jones. He currently resides in Brooklyn, New York and works at Long Island University.

.

www.ingramcontent.com/pod-product-compliance
Lightning Source LLC
LaVergne TN
LVHW021508080426
835509LV00018B/2440